Please State the Nature of Your Nature of Your Emergency

Aaron Anstett

Sagging Shorts

Some of these poems originally appeared in *Scoundrel Time*.

© 2017 by Aaron Anstett

All Rights Reserved.

Set in Williams Caslon Text with LaTeX.

ISBN: 978-1-944697-52-5 (paperback)
ISBN: 978-1-944697-53-2 (ebook)
Library of Congress Control Number: 2017949818

Sagging Meniscus Press
saggingmeniscus.com

I believe in America.

—Mario Puzo, *The Godfather*

Can we stand ditches.
Can we mean well.
Do we talk together.
Have we red cross.
A great many people speak of feet.
And socks.

—Gertrude Stein, "America"

Contents

Final Animal	1
Against All Evidence	2
Almanac	3
Next Election	4
Things We Say	6
I Came Here Looking for Something	8
Autumn Morning in Philadelphia	9
Other Weather	10
A Gap Where Things and People Once Had Been	11
The Beginnings of Sorrows	12
Last Will	13
Autumn Leaves Tattered as Abandoned Amusement Park Awnings	14
Insert Here Lengthy Disclaimer	16
Smoke in the Wind's Inscrutable Scribble	18
Alternative Facts	20
The Collective Is Unlikely or Always the Same Path from the Spigot to the Drain	21

Alternative Facts	22
Unexpected	23
Terrestrial Radio	24
Essential Dilemma	26
(unintelligible)	28
(unintelligible)	30
(unintelligible)	31
English Only	32
Gusty Winds Likely	33
Being of Sound	34
Commute	36
Alternative Facts	38
Sepia	39
Please State the Nature of Your Emergency	40
Facts Are Stumping Things	42
Things I Cannot	43
Other Than That, Mrs. Lincoln, How Did You Enjoy the Play?	44
Nothing Funny	45
Alternative Facts	46
The Tomorrow We Stumble Into	47
Oh,	48

PLEASE

STATE

THE

NATURE

OF

YOUR

EMERGENCY

Final Animal

Translucent amphibian or molecular
invertebrate, scavenging rodent

or stubborn ungulate, whatever
it is endures all manner of onslaught

for that imaginable unimaginable
forthcoming moment it's the last thing

blinking and breathing in landscape
covered with almost comical

numbers of corpses, largely us, no
one living to analyze prayer as a form

of fluid dynamics or correlate lightning
to astral anomalies, no one remembering

the famed island let alone its tavern
where painters slugged each other

and how much a beer and shot cost,
no recalling terraced squatters' shacks

of South America or the fact
ancient Egyptians believed frogs

emerged from flooding
and the coupling of land and water.

Against All Evidence

Because we cannot believe in God
the Monster entirely but believe in God
the Monster a little, we'll never be elected.

We own these souls. Won't someone
fix them, uncover and preserve forever
patches of sidewalk sun to sit in?

In this game we walk
our characters forward
and have no control over
what rushes toward us.

Caravaggio painted these faces
in 1607 and 1608 and 1610 respectively
then disappeared into history. How pretty
his features in concealed self-portraits.

Maybe I'll vote my subconscious this year,
Walking Scissors for mayor, *I-Don't-Want-
To-Kiss-a-Man-Yes-I-Do* for senator.

I must tell you my guess about God.

If the flooding continues, the lions, who swim,
could cross the moat and climb the walls.

Almanac

As seen in trees' interiors,
rings thin dry years, fatten wet.

Locals allow rain, leaves, snow descend
on everyone's grave but the murderer's.

What to do but gird and endure
our record-setting weather?

Landscapes gleam in sunset
orange as prison uniforms.

Maybe we'll start seeing
all things as the divine's emanation.

Who says what casts shadows
across our startled expressions?

Next Election

Maybe inject chlorophyll beneath skin to grow own food as we go.

Maybe clutch in each palm handfuls of fat as hedge against vanishing animals.

Maybe class up cursing with smattering of Latin.

Maybe drive to supermarket stunned by afternoon sun faint like photocopy of photocopy of photocopy of smudge, see-through against sky window-cleaner blue.

Maybe tell nice officer who asks we're operating under influence of symbolic aura, pale and vivid colors and dot-to-dot constellations we daylight take on faith.

Maybe hope at last our suffering possesses the symmetry of Dante.

Maybe lie on courthouse sidewalk reciting petition drafted first by inscribing in bartop whiskey puddle the symbol for infinity.

Maybe recall crows wheeling in sunset over dollar store.

Maybe move lips while reading novel whose plot points magic and spells resolve.

Maybe remember Melville wrote *Moby-Dick* in western Massachusetts near whale-shaped hill.

Maybe imagine mansplaining the ways of God to man.

Maybe compose libretto for opera buffa celebrating domestic life, *La Dolce Rigmarole*.

Maybe make claims drastic and hyperbolic: neutrinos inoculate flesh against spontaneous combustion, one example, and each instance comes at us at the same velocity: suddenly.

Things We Say

After latest tragedy, let's drift
asleep listing words for what
fish, oblivious in waters, do:
Plunge, glide, dive, sway.

Our daily allowance of banalities
includes again that strange phrase,
"realistic fiction."

Among many nevers:
Billionaire or seeing
through spider's ocelli.

As sidewalk sleeper dreams
of icy vodka careening
in bloodstream's arena,

as sea assails the shore
with shells, kelp, itself,

think of labor horses
perform in lyric
and actual, foam of lather
slicking necks.

Oh, bury me
like battle reenactor,
musket in casket.

Before then, let's,
you know, *it*,
on historical attraction.

Let's volunteer hours
overseeing elections.
This candidate believes everyone
deserves what happens.

I Came Here Looking for Something

On shadowed path before sudden, lumbering bear,
play dead or perform world's greatest trembling

aspen impression. Alive again in tent or cabin, sip
thimbles or saucepans of whiskey until moonlight

glints on all the pitchfork points inside you. Admit
that little's louder than God's silence. One day, full

of coffee and sorrow, maybe playing Buck Owens'
"Streets of Bakersfield" on repeat while reading fusty,

meticulous history of prosody, you'll say for their sounds
"behemoth," "jacaranda." Who wouldn't go back to be born

in hospital named for cigarette brand or despot or become
insect drifting like hammock napper, ferried in dent of wind?

Autumn Morning in Philadelphia

I choose to believe the evidence
of a world before or after I'm in it
hoax and fake as some have claimed
dinosaur bones and fossils, salted
across the earth by God to test our faith.

Yet all over this city mothers serenade babies
in many languages and in the courtyard
around Independence Hall chestnut and elm
leaves fall in patterns never the exact same again,
large as the parchment of historical documents.

Other Weather

Solve the climate crisis with this one weird trick.
You'll never believe what happens next.

Gap Where Things and People Once Had Been

This museum object label called by curators "tombstone" fails
to list dust and color-dulling sun among the artists' materials.
We hazarded a guess at price at auction but grew distracted
estimating gallons per second evaporating in Amazon basin.
Maybe we'll redefine light years calculating square inches
of skin darkened then lit so many days then dividing by all eternity.
Will it help or hurt believing air a kind of flab we wallow through?
Seeing suffering, we flee everything, water tainted with prescription
and illicit drugs, shadows cast across asphalt by eolian litter divining
how we'll die, merlot and pineapple sunset, wood grain's and wood
smoke's ripples, waves with grit in them. Likely we'll never hear
the ruffle and flutter of paparazzi shutters, us the apertures' objects,
gate number something or other, LAX or PEK or elsewhere. In distance
of earliest existence, our origins' elements linger: river and brick, stream
and stick, two strangers' bright idea. Fine print stipulates rain one day
pinpoints us, x-y coordinates toward which so much descends.

The Beginnings of Sorrows

In my country, number one
    for billionaires, prisoners, franchises
offer menu consistency. What lies
    dormant today in the collective
unconscious? Akin to tintype, sun prints
    itself on structures and skin.
As we age our vocabularies
    expand, contract with names of maladies,
despots, lands next for neglect.
    Never so many in history displaced
and in transit, our weather's breaking
    records again. In maps, see crimson,
scarlet, ruby, ochre, folly, wine,
    rust auguring sea level rise
and agricultural loss. Whom,
    in interminable funeral, transcend
time's passing imagining nude?
    How hope some ideal elsewhere,
mirroring correspondence, spooky
    action at a distance, perfects
all motion? In my country,
    stick's best trick: stay stuck
years marking spot sprung culprit
    returns to at long last as salmon
and tangerine sunset tints the earth.

Last Will

What will the children say if I say I fear
our fates are decided in secret meetings
and my best advice remains ignore
many things, maniacal yowling and floating

casino's calliope? Bequest? Avoid these accidents:
Committee chair or huddled under trestle,
wondering which hinge reddest, rustiest,
most sunset among world's abandoned

amusement parks, every continent, machinery
grease long ago evaporated. An animal urge
overwhelms to confirm the taste of dust and blood
then wince hearing screech and squeak. Insert

description. Append assertion. Let imagination drift
and memory steer. Remember your mother, shape
of her face yelling and yawning, looking
blank, pretending not to hear a solitary word.

Autumn Leaves Tattered as Abandoned Amusement Park Awnings

For bargains in heartache
try liquor store or mall.
You enter through
you-size hole in wall.

Pay with worry, currency
flooding market. In public
parks, see sun-struck,
gaudy desperations on spared
and sun-aged faces
as living symbols
for yearning, aching.

It's hard to argue the good
work clouds do, pivotal
to water's distribution, resembling
little other than animals
and iffy outlines of big ideas.

Who yelled in cadence
at midnight in February,
on Grand Central steps,
blocking entry?

"I'm hungry. I'm homeless. Please help me."
"I'm hungry. I'm homeless. Please help me."
"I'm hungry. I'm homeless. Please help me."

Next morning a figure
looking like 19th century
etching illustration
for exhibition of wild men
rocked on subway bench,
repeating so earnestly it sounded
both prayer and cursing, "It's freedom
of speech. America. America.
Amerigo Vespucci."

Insert Here Lengthy Disclaimer

Daylight in cinder block tavern a drunk
man said he killed his friend in accident
on accident driving into tree and went to corrections.

After umpteenth drink he said this
as the jukebox played the sad, slow songs
you imagine and on the television potential
contestants jumped around hopeful in costumes.

There's a hole in the bucket. With what will I fix it?

Nobody there cares if you're thirsty.
Nobody cares if you've eaten.

A man-shaped cloud of mayflies appears
to operate tilt-a-whirl in Iowa river
town murky summer evening in memory.

Answers vary by region, how many
syllables in "fire" and "wheel." Nothing
of our substance remains as-is, but orbits

of atoms and particles persist, those circuits,
as microscopic and monstrous animals
navigate volumes of water. All matter

serves as units of measure: universe,
whisker, planet, satellite, tooth, box springs
and mattresses burning along avenues, stacks
of axles and tires fenced by train tracks.

Dear Arresting Officer, No joke:
How do we endure?

I ordered another, pledging allegiance
to my regular, The Never Enough.

Smoke in the Wind's Inscrutable Scribble

The abandoned U.S. Army base
intact under layers of Greenland ice
surfaces blurry then focuses faster.

In absence of evidence, the heavens humble.

At outdoor music festival,
pesticides sold as party drugs
stun, blunt and sharpen
sun and sunset.

Then an expanse of skin indicates where
earth's curvature should be considered
among uncountable nouns:

luggage	blood	oxygen
dust	porcelain	rice
biology	harm	money
water	wool	scenery

Imagine ancestors puzzled what
animal the sky was.

In clear weather, 1,100 feet is the maximum
distance to contemplate the plausible
crimes within lifetime: Heist,
then grand theft, then homicide.

In land overrun with animatronic vermin,
calculate refraction given decreasing visibility.

A colorful sky is often due to scattering of light off particles as
    in this photograph of sunset.

Competing with machine's spatial cognition,
perhaps we'll verify procedures in bomb-defusing manual,
then calibrate degrees of realism mapping detritus's flight
    paths.

Maybe fake own deaths in Philippines,
open manila envelope and confirm certificate
given candidate reality
performer prone to rhetorical flourishes.

More and more I like the natural
order less and less.

Too late, I fear, to feign a life-
long interest in currency misprints

and what a president says
in a crazy person's head.

Alternative Facts

For five seasons in the 1970s, Noam Chomsky ghostwrote scripts for *Hee Haw*, the country-music variety show, though the long-rumored affair with Minnie Pearl has never been confirmed.

The Collective Is Unlikely or Always the Same Path from the Spigot to the Drain

Old tropical sunrises failed travelers.
After the riots, the buzz was striking.
Dawn keeps surroundings naked.
A carpenter sheaths it in copper and a mixture of
    wonderful colors.
Electrified blood thrums.
A gas station projects ideas, but one senses that
    silence shapes eyelids.

Night lifts mystery.
Enormous to-do, thank you.
Sleeve circles stir evening avenues, a down-at-heels
    cinema.
Words blur racetrack fast.
Eyes swallow ripples, moon in shadowy ditches.
In the future, new trees refurbish the square as the
    gaze erases nature's end.

Alternative Facts

As with a duck's quack, a policeman's baton striking a skull produces no echo.

Unexpected

admins empty the office
and stack by a side door belongings:
camping chair, maps, aquarium

no breeze through tresses
no pant suits
no dresses

no sun and sunglasses

no recalling the deceased as ever
in Central or South American
ravine beset by small and arboreal
eyelash vipers that occupy
a wide range of colors

or as walker who loved the undersides
of powerlines and branches
lit by passing ambulances

Terrestrial Radio

My 12:00 a.m. Waffle House cook
asks how's my hash browns then
offers in the titty bars around Tampa
guys with guitars sing Jimmy Buffet
all night and day and if you say
one bad word you better run
north to NY or PA.

A radio report claims a mouse's face
provides sufficient surface to support
100 ticks that spread a pestilence.

How to inventory the infinitesimal
among all matter's iterative existence,
each thing the infinite's mean, each
its means, even every intersection
in which precipitation in the form
of ephemeral ice and snow pile up,
forming pileups galore. An auto
and sentence disassemble, meaning
meaning dissembles.

Asking just a touch
in cup and check,
I clamor for a black
hole to provide us passage
to other, better planet.

Essential Dilemma

Man the only animal
argues yes/no animal

and which the body's
essential dilemma, each

bit its expiration, strung
with nerves, fraught in general,

says, too, praise the intricate,
difficult work of blood vessels,

galaxies, atoms. Praise
ancestors struggled up

from forlorn saltwater.
Praise all matter

rubbed between fingerprints
eventually granules.

*

Loitering at intersection,
teetering as wind

confettis grit—eyes,
ears, lips—feeling nervous

system like flowering umbrella,
how in so much eavesdrop

accurately and glean
from speaker's blurry

features which: *Museum*
on *fire* or *Museum* of *fire*?

*

Filmed slow-motion in daylight, opulence of disaster.
Night: time-lapse tracery, stars' and headlights' longhand.

(unintelligible)

Oh I'm seeing numbers
twenty four billion I think
I'll do it for ten billion
or less that's not a lot
of money relative
to what we're talking
about if we stop one
percent of the drugs
from coming in
and we'll stop
all of it but if we
stop one percent
of the drugs because
we have the wall
they're coming around
in certain areas but if
you have a wall they can't
do it because it's a real
wall that's a tremendously
good investment one percent
the drugs pouring through
on the southern border
are unbelievable we're
becoming a drug culture
there's so much and
most of it's coming

from the southern
border the wall will
stop the drugs I think
ten billion or less
and if I do a super-duper
higher better better
security everything else
maybe it goes a little
bit more but it's
not going to be anywhere
near kind of numbers
and they're using those
numbers they're using
the high numbers to make
it sound impalatable and
the fact it's going
to cost much less
money just like the airplane
I told you about which
I hope you can write about

(unintelligible)

This is risk that's involved, because if
the missile goes off and goes in a city
or goes in a civilian area—you know
the boats were hundreds of miles away—
and if this missile goes off and lands
in the middle of a town or a hamlet every
decision is much harder than you'd normally
make this is involving death and life and so
many things so it's far more responsibility
the financial cost of everything is so massive
every agency this is thousands of times bigger
the United States than the biggest company
in the world you know you go down the list

(unintelligible)

Look he turned down many coal ships
these massive coal ships are coming
where they get a lot of their income
They're coming into China
and they're being turned away
That's never happened before
The fuel, the oil, so many different things
You saw the editorial they had
in their paper saying they cannot
be allowed to have nuclear you know et cetera
People have said they've never seen this
ever before in China we have the same relationship
with others there's a great foundation that's built
great foundation and I think it's going
to produce tremendous results for our country

English Only

Zero algebra.

Zero lilac, zero orange, zero lime, zero lemon.
Zero apricot. Zero artichoke.

Coffee! Candy! Alcohol!

Zero mattress.

Zero cotton.

Zero satin.

Gusty Winds Likely

Say trembling highway signs.

Being of Sound

> "I've got these arms and legs that flipflop, flipflop!"
> Pere Ubu, "Navvy"

Goodbye alpine meadows, goodbye
the ultimate in live nude extravaganzas.
Goodbye moonlight on burglar's crowbar,
goodbye sunlight on rusty screen door.
Goodbye numbers and all their variants.
Goodbye critters, goodbye varmints.
Goodbye water. Goodbye land.
Goodbye foggy notions, and lucky
guesses, I'll miss you most.
Goodbye rain and goodbye roofs.
Goodbye glint and goodbye glare.
Goodbye noon. Goodbye false dawn.
Goodbye officers and goodbye miscreants.

I've said the ugliest and prettiest
things I felt and felt no better
after, either, something in me ill
at ease, quivery, living.

All my life I labor to stymie
the body's ouster of the so-called soul.

Count me among occupants of alleys in which such ilk eke,
among burned books in which the exact word lurked.

While able I'll
inhale chemical,
forestall nightfall,
wrestle jackal,
Australian crawl waterfall,
wriggle ankle,
curtail rainfall,
whistle madrigal,
puzzle know-it-all,
banana peel automobile,
eyeball fireball,
kindle rubble,
unveil pinhole,
unspool molecule,
overrule minuscule,
distill vitriol,
overhaul the overall,
crank call all you-all.

Commute

Oh, my compatriots, you follow
too closely in oversized vehicles.

The moon swells and thins,
gleams, dims, rises, lowers.

The new old sun glowers
on guard rails, us, big
box store parking lots.

I cannot see more
than seconds of faces.

The radio report says scientists say
of shoe laces they loosen
through gravity and movement.

When will I feel magical
as Marx thought capital?

When I drive by pasture's speckle
of wide-hipped, thin-ribbed cattle,
eating green so green
it's chemical and miracle?

Weather says so.

My brain says so.

Science says so
what, my brain
was built to save
itself, to say
to the containing body,
My say so: Hide, run.

For relief from many afflictions
I pray to pronoun whose referent drifts.

Then I yearn to name insects
Eurydice, Orpheus, depending,
any absurd effort, maybe
catalog terrible ways to be
woken: prodded
by nightstick or boot.

Trouble follows on schedule,
little by little by little.

Alternative Facts

Water freezes instantly on contact with the president's scrotum, encasing it in a fragile, craquelure shell.

Sepia

Where would I not look?

On forest floor, in darkest woods, improbable spittoon!

That hope the thinnest,
stiffest rope a phony swami shimmies.

Please State the Nature of Your Emergency

Whatever suffering we have coming,
some among us deduce huge, unseen
planets from objects' warped orbits.

On the many channels, no answer.

Imagine each dawn and dusk
the aftermath of some god's
vast wrist flick,

then think of all the streets
and blame the light
for making visible litter
of leaves and paper wrappers.

Graves await their claimants,
but please do not construe
the beautiful, open air as invitation.

Consider all the air the lungs
must share and sort,
the water blood becomes,

the tired surprise
of anyone's death
a kind of sunrise.

History happens while we clean
clothes and dishes, worn
from many labors.

But you were talking
about the phenomena
of snow and thunder,
fresh patch interrupted
by succinct blood drop.

Across mountains fog
renders other,
ellipses of birds flicker.

Angry, I forget exist
beaches feet score,
lines strung between windows
from which clothes drip
water to a street

and stack of red bricks
around lamppost on corner
near car equal to annual pay.

How quickly life can change.

Facts Are Stumping Things

In government by stunt
recall the verb to eat like animals
flesh from which we're estranged
then remember we're meat that makes
us strange and wonder which of many
its is one *its* referent: whole people or insect
on arm slapped somewhere in sepia.

While evils are sufferable, ask a gullible uncle
to circle in documents names of our enemies.

Then select the range of years
from which to read daily a paper
and pretend now's then.

Then maybe go *en masse* to that thin
sliver, Togo, then solo north to Burkina Faso.

Things I Cannot

"Good sleeping weather"
we said rickety mornings
watching rain through plate glass.
X-number poisons by something a.m.
made sense, and for prayer,
Let the prisoner use birthmark
as landmark, ascend ladder of spittle,
and smokers huddle outside hospitals. Amen.

*

In latest *Motel* motel
a mother wakes

supposing the mind's aura
and color harpsichord arpeggios.

Temperatures fix gutter slush in place.
Outlines in dust and grasses, aftermath

of bodies, weapons, detail an alphabet.
Go forth and spell place names on the planet.

Other Than That, Mrs. Lincoln, How Did You Enjoy the Play?

A pig that good you don't eat all at once.
You might need to pet him first.
They like to think they're the only ones up here.
All we had to do was switch the heads.

You might need to pet him first.
We need the eggs.
All we had to do was switch the heads.
Someone has stolen our tent.

We need the eggs.
That's not a duck.
Someone has stolen our tent.
I'm telling everyone.

That's not a duck.
A pig that good you don't eat all at once.
I'm telling everyone.
They like to think they're the only ones up here.

Nothing Funny

> "It takes the corrupt, ectoplasmic shape of a prayer
> Or money, that connects with a government somewhere."
> Edwin Denby, "The Shoulder"

What to quip about the president's
budget moving wealth from poor to rich
as in the waiting areas cable channel
news crawls name the places latest
troubled loner shooters surface
between pharmaceutical commercials?

One headline: "Thanks to crushing
medical debt, crowdfunding sites boom."

Better to imagine all the waters
composing snow or argue
plant and animal cells more
action than location, less
substance than function.

A neighbor has posted a photograph:
Shelves and orderly jars of soil,
each labeled with name of victim,
glass housing silt and twigs.

Alternative Facts

The plural of *the* is *these*, the plural of *of* is *ooves*, the plural of *plural* is *pleated*.

The Tomorrow We Stumble Into

In aimless and meaningless universe, our existence
improbably occurs, given statistics.

Circling the earth glide myriad instruments
diagnosing conditions from numerous distances.

Long last, after so very much of it,
we remember the lessons of history:

    a. Levels of damage: Bad, Worse, Horrific.
    b. Never invade Russia in winter.

With some number number 2 pencils let's draft petitions
against waste and abuse in graphite and timber industries

then squander years steeping selves in moon-landing conspiracies
and cataloging sorrow, frivolity, and death-metal taxonomies.

Museum of Invisible Scripture, pamphlets hand-written in vinegar
react to heat, then words appear, urgent, the color of tea.

Oh,

each object hurt
les to a future, ur
ges into its ow
n vanishing.

That eventual then, when
the brain's the iddest
ever, thoughts scurry
like emergency
services personnel, no?

I like my prayers make-do, homely,
fashioned from the at-hand.

To quell all fugitive feelings,
I watch footage of the rich
indulging in luxury products
then dream of the cryptozoological as if
the sight of them might slow diseases.

Leaves flicker to their shadows
past statue in courtyard,
general of battle whose cause
no one living recalls.

Remember the painting in Italy, St. Jerome
clapping and weeping over his doll-like Jesus?

In the office, behold:
light rays splintered
by thin tip of thumb tack.

If only my work all day
were contemplating the voluminous
output of Anonymous.

I feel great love and pity for people
plural, though one by one they irk.

Who from bridge to river
falls so many Mississippis?

Now let's tell
the saddest stories.
You start.

(An open parenthetical ends the poem

Aaron Anstett's previous collections are *Moreover, Insofar as Heretofore, Each Place the Body's, No Accident,* and *Sustenance.* He lives in Colorado with his wife, Lesley, and children.

Photo by Lesley Ginsberg

www.ingramcontent.com/pod-product-compliance
Lightning Source LLC
Chambersburg PA
CBHW051703040426
42446CB00009B/1273